AF228517

SAN ANTONIO SPURS

BY DREW SILVERMAN

SportsZone
An Imprint of Abdo Publishing
abdobooks.com

abdobooks.com

Published by Abdo Publishing, a division of ABDO, PO Box 398166, Minneapolis, Minnesota 55439. Copyright © 2023 by Abdo Consulting Group, Inc. International copyrights reserved in all countries. No part of this book may be reproduced in any form without written permission from the publisher. SportsZone™ is a trademark and logo of Abdo Publishing.

Printed in China.
052022
092022

Cover Photo: Eric Gay/AP Images
Interior Photos: Melinda Nagy/Shutterstock Images, 1; Timothy A. Clary/AFP/Getty Images, 4; Darren Abate/AP Images, 6; David J. Phillip/AP Images, 9, 11; Focus on Sport/Getty Images Sport/Getty Images, 12, 24, 34; Focus on Sport/Getty Images, 14; Dan Levine/AFP/Getty Images, 16; David Zalubowski/AP Images, 18; Anne Heisenfelt/AP Images, 20; Ronald Cortes/Getty Images Sport/Getty Images, 23; Mitchell Layton/Getty Images Sport/Getty Images, 27; Brett Coomer/AP Images, 29; Chris Covatta/Getty Images Sport/Getty Images, 30, 41; Tony Dejak/AP Images, 31; Craig Mitchelldyer/AP Images, 33; Mark Lennihan/AP Images, 37; Ronald Martinez/Getty Images Sport/Getty Images, 39

Editor: Charlie Beattie
Series Designer: Joshua Olson

Library of Congress Control Number: 2021951665

Publisher's Cataloging-in-Publication Data

Names: Silverman, Drew, author.
Title: San Antonio Spurs / by Drew Silverman
Description: Minneapolis, Minnesota : Abdo Publishing, 2023 | Series: Inside the NBA | Includes online resources and index.
Identifiers: ISBN 9781532198441 (lib. bdg.) | ISBN 9781098272098 (ebook)
Subjects: LCSH: San Antonio Spurs (Basketball team)--Juvenile literature. | Basketball--Juvenile literature. | Professional sports--Juvenile literature. | Sports franchises--Juvenile literature.
Classification: DDC 796.32364--dc23

Contents

CHAPTER ONE

LEONARD BREAKS OUT

The San Antonio Spurs needed a boost. It was Game 3 of the 2014 National Basketball Association (NBA) Finals, and the Spurs were going up against the star-studded Miami Heat. San Antonio had a veteran lineup. Yet it was one of the team's youngest players who stepped up.

The Heat were loaded with star power. LeBron James, one of the greatest basketball players of all time, was in his prime. Fellow All-Stars Dwyane Wade and Chris Bosh were among the best at their positions too. And that "Big Three" had led Miami to the previous two NBA titles—beating the Spurs in the 2013 Finals.

It was a heartbreaking loss for the Spurs. One year later, and once again meeting the Heat for the championship, San Antonio was out for revenge.

San Antonio Spurs forward Kawhi Leonard throws down a dunk against the Miami Heat during the 2014 NBA Finals.

Leonard, *far left*, was the perfect complement to San Antonio's veteran stars, *from right*, Tony Parker, Manu Ginobili, and Tim Duncan.

While Miami grabbed many of the headlines, the Spurs had several great players as well. Tim Duncan was one of the best power forwards in basketball history. Tony Parker and Manu Ginobili formed a dynamic duo at the guard position. All three had won multiple NBA championships in San Antonio. And all three were over the age of 30—Duncan was 38, Ginobili was 36, and Parker was 32.

Small forward Kawhi Leonard couldn't match their experience. At 22 years old, he was younger than all but one other member of the team. But Leonard had been a big part of the Spurs' balanced offense during the season. Starting

65 games, he averaged 12.8 points while often playing shutdown defense.

Fans were eager for the heavyweight rematch for the NBA title. The teams traded the first two games, with San Antonio winning Game 1 and falling in Game 2. Leonard struggled in those games, scoring only 18 total points. Before Game 3, reporters asked him about his play so far.

"I've just got to be more aggressive on both ends of the floor and help my team win," he said.

HOT START

Leonard wasted no time turning his words into action. On the Spurs' third possession of the game, the 6-foot-7-inch wing drove to the basket. He got fouled and made both free throws. Less than two minutes later, Leonard drove the lane again. The Heat fouled him again, but this time he managed to flip in an off-balance shot. With Leonard sinking the free throw, San Antonio had an early 11–8 lead.

Leonard was just getting started. The next time the Spurs had the ball, he threw down a

Cruise Control

In the 2014 NBA Finals, all four of the Spurs' victories came by at least 15 points. In the Spurs' only loss in the series, they were narrowly defeated 98–96. Over the five games, San Antonio outscored Miami by 70 points.

two-handed breakaway dunk. One minute later, he added a
three-pointer. It put San Antonio up 18–10. Miami had to call a
timeout and regroup.

On the Heat's second possession after the timeout, Leonard
added a defensive gem. As the ultra-athletic James drove
to the basket, Leonard smothered his layup attempt with
both hands.

With 5:33 left in the opening quarter, Leonard swished
another three-pointer. His 13 points were more than Miami had
as a team. The Spurs were up 25–12.

It was already a breakout game for the young forward, but
he wasn't done. In the final minute of the first quarter, Spurs
guard Patty Mills found Leonard open in the corner. James
closed on him with his hand high to distract a shot. It didn't
bother the Spurs forward. As James moved in, Leonard shot
over him and hit again.

FINISHING STRONG

Leonard's final first-quarter point total was 16. He was 5-for-5
from the field and hit all three of his free throws. The Spurs led
41–25. Led by its youngest star, San Antonio was routing Miami.
At halftime the score was 71–50 in favor of the Spurs. But Miami
charged back. With less than eight minutes left in the game,
San Antonio's lead was down to 90–80. The Heat had a chance

Leonard followed up his Game 3 performance with 20 points in Game 4 and 22 in the series-clinching Game 5.

to pull off an amazing comeback victory. That's when Leonard stepped up again.

On the Spurs' next possession, he drove the baseline for a one-handed dunk. The next time down the floor he was fouled, and he knocked down both shots. On the next trip, Leonard passed to Parker, who drilled a three-pointer. The Spurs, now leading 97–82, were back in control.

The final score was 111–92. In his outstanding performance, Leonard made 10 of 13 shots and six of seven free throws.

Over his three NBA seasons, Leonard had never scored more than 26 points in any game. He poured in 29 in Game 3. And he was just heating up.

MVP

The young forward was suddenly unstoppable. Two days later he had 20 points and 14 rebounds in Game 4. Among them was a thunderous, two-hand put-back dunk off a missed three-pointer in the second quarter. The Spurs cruised to a 107–86 win.

Young and Hungry

Leonard was two weeks from his twenty-third birthday when he was named Finals MVP in 2014. Only one player had ever won it at a younger age. Earvin "Magic" Johnson of the Los Angeles Lakers actually beat Leonard's record twice. He won it as a 20-year-old rookie in 1980. Johnson then did it again in 1982, when he was 22 years, 298 days old.

San Antonio needed only one more win to secure a championship. In Game 5, Leonard delivered again. The Spurs trailed by 16 points early in the game. But a powerful performance from Leonard helped them fight back. With 4:50 left in the second quarter, Leonard's three-pointer gave San Antonio a 37–35 lead. It was the Spurs' first lead of the game, and they never trailed again. Leonard finished with a team-high 22 points. He also led the Spurs with 10 rebounds.

Leonard accepts the Finals MVP trophy from NBA legend Bill Russell after the Spurs' five-game victory over the Heat.

Most importantly, the 104–87 victory sparked championship celebrations in San Antonio.

Afterward, Leonard was named the Most Valuable Player (MVP) of the series. During the Finals, he averaged 17.8 points per game. He made 61.2 percent of his shots, including 57.9 percent of his three-pointers. Leonard also played tough defense on James, the MVP in each of the previous two Finals.

"Right now, it's just surreal to me," Leonard said after winning the award. "I had a great group of guys behind me."

The Finals win was San Antonio's fifth since 1999. Duncan had been a part of every one of those victories. Parker and Ginobili had been members of the championship teams in 2003, 2005, and 2007. They might not have added another one in 2014, however, without the rising star now riding with them.

AN ANTONIO
35
bullets
11

CHAPTER TWO

THE PATH TO GREATNESS

The San Antonio Spurs were not always known by that name. And they had not always played in the NBA. In fact, the franchise debuted in Dallas in 1967. At the time, the team was known as the Dallas Chaparrals. They played in an 11-team league called the American Basketball Association (ABA).

The Chaparrals were not popular in Dallas. In 1970–71 they tried playing in other cities around Texas. They even changed their name to the Texas Chaparrals. One new home, Fort Worth, was close by. The other, Lubbock, was five hours away. The idea did not work. After one season, the team returned to Dallas full time.

In 1973 the Chaparrals' owners moved the team south to San Antonio and changed the team's name to the Spurs. Three years after that, in 1976, the ABA merged with the NBA. As part of the merger agreement, the NBA took in four ABA teams.

During his five seasons with the Spurs, forward Larry Kenon averaged 20.7 points per game.

George Gervin scored more than 23,000 points in a San Antonio uniform.

As a result, the New York Nets, Denver Nuggets, Indiana Pacers, and San Antonio Spurs moved to the more established league.

San Antonio was competitive right away in its new league. Led by high-scoring guard George Gervin, the Spurs made the playoffs in their first seven NBA seasons. Five times in that stretch, they won their division. Although San Antonio reached the conference finals three times, the team never got over the hump. Twice the Spurs were beaten by the powerhouse Los Angeles Lakers. After losing to Los Angeles in the 1983 Western Conference finals, the Spurs did not have another winning record for seven years.

ARRIVAL OF THE ADMIRAL

The stagnant team needed a change up. Gervin was traded to the Chicago Bulls before the 1985–86 season. The Spurs still had good players on their roster. Small forward Mike Mitchell was a productive scorer. Center Artis Gilmore was a force down low. Shooting guard Alvin Robertson was a defensive specialist who could also provide offense. However, the team struggled without Gervin.

San Antonio sunk to a 28–54 record in 1986–87. But good news was on the way. The Spurs won the NBA Draft lottery after the season, meaning they got to pick first. "It's the greatest thing that could have happened to us," general manager Bob Bass said. "There's no doubt in my mind that

David Robinson led the NBA in rebounding during the 1990–91 season and in blocked shots during the 1991–92 season. He also won a scoring title in 1993–94.

we'll take Robinson." And indeed they did. The Spurs used the pick on center David Robinson from the United States Naval Academy.

"The Admiral," as Robinson was known, had to spend the next two years in the Navy. For the Spurs, his NBA arrival was worth the wait. The Spurs also picked up other talented players like forwards Terry Cummings and Sean Elliott. But it was Robinson's arrival in 1989–90 that started a San Antonio turnaround. The Spurs finished 56–26 and were just one win away from reaching the conference finals. The 7-foot-1-inch Robinson was named Rookie of the Year.

Robinson's career continued to blossom in the mid-1990s. The center became one of the NBA's best scorers. And San Antonio once again was a regular contender. But the team still struggled to navigate the tough Western Conference playoffs. San Antonio won at least 47 games each year through the 1995–96 season. But it reached the Western Conference finals only once. In 1995 the Spurs were beaten in six games by the eventual champion Houston Rockets.

A GOOD YEAR FOR A BAD YEAR

During the 1996–97 season, Robinson struggled with injuries. The Spurs played without their star in 76 of their 82 games. Additionally, Elliott missed 43 games due to injury. The result was a 20–62 record, the worst in franchise history.

The miserable season came at a perfect time for the Spurs. Two things happened that set in motion the best stretch in franchise history.

First, general manager Gregg Popovich fired coach Bob Hill in December 1996. Popovich took over as Hill's replacement. Then, after the season, the Spurs were back in the draft lottery. Though they had the third-worst record in the league,

The pairing of the veteran Robinson, *left*, with young star Tim Duncan gave the Spurs a nearly unstoppable duo in the paint.

they won the top pick again. The prize was another star big man. San Antonio snatched center Tim Duncan from Wake Forest University.

"Oh, what an opportunity for us," Spurs owner Peter Holt said after his team won the lottery. "We already have a great team, and [now we can] add someone like Tim Duncan? I mean, the world is our oyster."

Duncan and Robinson meshed perfectly. Instantly, the "Twin Towers" put the Spurs back on top. And Popovich proved a perfect fit on the sidelines. In the first season with Robinson and Duncan, Popovich guided San Antonio to a 56–26 record and a series win in the playoffs.

THE DYNASTY BEGINS

The 1998–99 season was San Antonio's breakthrough. The Spurs defeated the New York Knicks in five games to claim the first NBA championship in team history. Veteran guard Avery Johnson made the winning shot in the final minute of Game 5. Duncan, in just his second NBA season, was named Finals MVP.

"It's just starting to soak in," Robinson said that night. "Boy, it's been a long journey. It's a joy, man. It's worth every minute of the journey."

That journey, it turned out, was just getting started. The 1998–99 season was shortened because of an NBA lockout. San Antonio finished 37–13 and capped off the year with its first-ever NBA championship. The next year the NBA went back to an 82-game schedule. The Spurs' win total jumped to 53. That started a streak of 18 consecutive 50-win seasons. With Duncan and Popovich leading the way, the Spurs became the NBA's model of consistency.

Tony Parker (9), Manu Ginobili (20), and Tim Duncan (21) are the only Spurs players to have appeared in more than 1,000 games for the team.

Robinson's final season came in 2002–03. He was no longer a dominant center. His scoring dipped to under 10 points per game for the first time in his career as he dealt with a bad back. But the Spurs sent him out on a high note by winning a second NBA title. This time the victory came in six games over the New Jersey Nets.

BECOMING A POWER

Two young players emerged during the second championship season. French point guard Tony Parker started all 82 games as a 20-year-old. And after previously playing overseas, Argentine shooting guard Manu Ginobili was a key bench player during his first NBA season.

Together with Duncan, the two international stars formed the core of the team for the next decade. San Antonio captured titles again in 2005 and 2007. The first came in seven games over the Detroit Pistons. The second came in a four-game sweep of the Cleveland Cavaliers.

"This is like a dream," Parker said after winning the 2007 championship. "I don't want to wake up."

Despite continued success, the team needed six more years to get back to the NBA Finals. The Spurs looked set for another title in 2013 against the Miami Heat. They led Game 6 in the final seconds before a three-pointer from Miami's Ray Allen tied the game. A victory would have won the series for San Antonio. But Miami prevailed in overtime. The Heat then took Game 7. It was the first time the Spurs had ever lost an NBA Finals.

The Highs and Lows

In 2015–16 the Spurs set a franchise record for wins, finishing 67–15. The roster featured Tim Duncan, Tony Parker, Manu Ginobili, Kawhi Leonard, and LaMarcus Aldridge. However, the Spurs were upset by Kevin Durant and the Oklahoma City Thunder in the second round of the playoffs.

The two teams met again the next year, with San Antonio coming out on top. A new star emerged for the Spurs in the series. Third-year small forward Kawhi Leonard was named Finals MVP. He looked set to take the reins as the team's star as the three veterans grew older. Duncan retired after the 2015–16 season. Ginobili followed him after the 2017–18 season. Parker left the team that same summer as a free agent.

A NEW ERA

Surprisingly, Leonard also left the team. He spent most of the 2017–18 season fighting with Spurs management over how he should treat a lingering leg injury. The disagreement spilled over into the off-season, and Leonard was traded to the Toronto Raptors in the summer of 2018.

Popovich managed to guide the team into the playoffs for one more season thanks to LaMarcus Aldridge and the addition of forward DeMar DeRozan. But San Antonio's postseason streak stopped in 2019–20. The NBA's model of consistency was absent from the playoffs for the first time since 1996–97.

Popovich stayed on as head coach as he approached the NBA's all-time wins record. But he had to do it with a new group of young players led by guard Dejounte Murray. For the first time in nearly three decades, the Spurs were starting over.

Spurs guard Dejounte Murray (5) drives past Tyrese Maxey of the Philadelphia 76ers during a game in January 2022.

CHAPTER THREE

STARS OF SAN ANTONIO

The Spurs didn't have many fans when they were still the Dallas Chaparrals. But those who did show up to the games got to see the team's first star. Guard James Silas was signed in 1972 and played nine seasons for the Chaparrals/Spurs in two different leagues. A solid scorer, he earned the nickname "the Late Mr. Silas" after hitting a number of game-winning fourth-quarter shots. He was the first Spurs player ever to have his jersey number retired by the team.

Joining Silas in 1974 was small forward George Gervin. Nicknamed "the Iceman" for his cool demeanor on the court, Gervin was one of the best scorers in ABA and NBA history. His specialty was the finger-roll shot, which he seemed to be able to execute whenever he wanted.

When the Spurs switched leagues, Gervin took the NBA by storm. In five seasons, from 1977–78 to 1981–82, Gervin led the

James Silas was an ABA All-Star twice before moving to the NBA with the Spurs.

league in scoring four times. And he did it with a style that was laid back and effortless. Opposing coach Dick Motta once said of Gervin, "You don't stop George Gervin. You just hope that his arm gets tired after 40 shots."

THE ADMIRAL

Before Duncan, Parker, and Ginobili arrived in San Antonio, the team was built around Hall of Famer David Robinson. The 7-foot-1-inch center was one of the NBA's giants from 1989 to 2003. But he wasn't always so large. As a junior in high school, Robinson was only 5 feet, 9 inches tall. He didn't even play basketball. He picked up the sport only as a senior, after he had grown 10 inches over the summer.

Quadruple Up

On February 18, 1986, Spurs shooting guard Alvin Robertson recorded one of only four quadruple-doubles in NBA history. Robertson had 20 points, 11 rebounds, 10 assists, and 10 steals against the Phoenix Suns.

Robinson kept growing after he joined the United States Naval Academy, which in sports just goes by Navy. By his sophomore year, he had reached 7 feet. He was also dominating on the court.

The Spurs picked him first overall in 1987, knowing Robinson couldn't play for them right away. All graduates of Navy have to serve two years of

active military service. But
Robinson proved worth
the wait once he got to the
NBA in 1989. At the time,
most big men lumbered
near the basket. Robinson
still had the athleticism of
a shorter player. And he
was also strong enough to
bully his way to the basket.
Back injuries slowed him
down later in his career.
But Robinson made the All-
Star team 10 times. He was
also the NBA MVP in 1995.

David Robinson throws up a hook shot against the Washington Bullets in December 1989.

COACH POP

The Spurs went through 11 head coaches in their first 21 NBA seasons. For the two and a half decades that followed, they had only one. Gregg Popovich was the Spurs' general manager in 1996 when the team was struggling. He decided to fire head coach Bob Hill and coach the team himself.

Popovich's motion offense made the Spurs one of the most unselfish teams in the league. All five players frequently touched the ball on each possession. Opponents found this approach difficult to stop. With clever players like Duncan,

Ginobili, and Parker under him, Popovich's Spurs were in contention for an NBA title seemingly every year.

On March 11, 2021, Popovich made history. He won his 1,336th regular-season game as the Spurs tipped the Utah Jazz 104–102. The victory set a new record for NBA head coaches.

THE BIG THREE

The "Big Three" was the nickname given to San Antonio's trio of stars during the 2000s and 2010s. Forward Tim Duncan and guards Tony Parker and Manu Ginobili made up the backbone of the team throughout its dynasty run.

While all three were legitimate stars, Duncan was the team's best player. He averaged at least 17.9 points and at least 10.1 rebounds in each of his first 13 seasons. Duncan also became an elite shot-blocker, a reliable passer, and an outstanding defender. For his simple style of play and his excellence in many areas, Duncan became known as "the Big Fundamental."

"He's not throwing behind-the-back passes, he's not doing tomahawk jams, he's not doing anything that's very flashy," veteran NBA coach Byron Scott said. "He's just a very unassuming guy who goes about his job, and the next thing you know he's got 23 points and 20 rebounds, like it's a normal day at the job."

Parker joined the team as a 19-year-old rookie before the 2001–02 season. Before Parker was drafted, Popovich put him through a workout with former NBA player Lance Blanks. The coach left the session thinking the 185-pound point guard wasn't tough enough for the NBA. Assistant general manager R. C. Buford had to convince Popovich to give Parker another try. The young guard changed Popovich's mind the second time around.

Parker was the perfect fit for San Antonio's offense. Most offenses feature the ball in the point guard's hands until a key pass is made. The Spurs under Popovich did not work that way. Dribbling was rare as they moved the ball with quick passes. That meant Parker picked up fewer assists than most point guards as the

Tim Duncan was the NBA regular-season MVP twice and won the NBA Finals MVP Award three times.

Tony Parker dished out 6,829 assists during his career with San Antonio.

ball was not always in his hands. But he was so quick that he could get loose from defenders without the ball. Parker could also beat almost anyone off the dribble when he needed to.

Ginobili spent the first three years after he was drafted playing professionally in Italy. He was already 25 years old when he joined the Spurs in 2002. That wasn't the only unusual thing about his amazing career. Unlike most star players, Ginobili spent a majority of his career coming off the bench. Of his more than 1,000 NBA games, he started only 349 of them. But he still scored like a starter. Ginobili averaged more than 13 points per game for his career. Many of them came on fearless drives to the basket. Ginobili popularized the "Euro step" move during his career. After he picked up his dribble near the basket, he took one step in one direction and a quick step back the other way. The move helped him evade defenders in tight spaces.

Together, the Big Three won four NBA championships. Duncan won five in all, helping the Spurs win a title before Parker and Ginobili joined the team. Combined, they earned 23 All-Star selections. Duncan alone made 15 All-Star teams—the most in Spurs history.

The Big Three had a rotating cast of supporting stars during their dynasty run. Sean Elliott was a key player on the 1999 championship team. He spent 11 of his 12 seasons in the NBA with the Spurs. Elliott is the eighth-leading scorer in franchise history. Point guard Avery Johnson also spent many years with San Antonio and helped the team win it all in 1999. Both Elliott and Johnson hit big shots during the Spurs' 1999 playoff run.

Spurs forward Bruce Bowen, *right*, made the NBA's All-Defensive team eight times during his career.

Bruce Bowen was a fixture on three title-winning teams during his stint with the Spurs from 2001 to 2009. During that time, Bowen was the team's defensive stopper as well as a reliable three-point shooter. He helped the Spurs win championships in 2003, 2005, and 2007.

THE NEW GENERATION

As the Big Three stars got older, the Spurs needed a new player to step up. That player was Kawhi Leonard. The small forward was acquired through a draft-day trade with the Indiana Pacers in 2011. Leonard then spent seven seasons with San Antonio.

During this time, Leonard made two All-Star teams and earned NBA Finals MVP honors in 2014. He was honored as the NBA's Defensive Player of the Year in 2015 and 2016. He became one of the most dominant two-way players of his generation.

Most NBA stars are picked near the top of the draft. But in the 2000s the Spurs had found great players lower down the order. Parker was taken twenty-eighth overall. Ginobili was picked in the second round. As those players moved on, the Spurs found more potential lower down the draft. Guard Dejounte Murray was the twenty-ninth pick in the 2016 draft. After spending two years on the bench and one recovering from a knee injury, he emerged as a reliable scorer.

In 2019 small forward Keldon Johnson was another twenty-ninth pick. He quickly became a go-to option for Popovich. Led by a new crop of young stars, the Spurs were looking to find the consistency that made them one of the NBA's best teams for two decades.

San Antonio forward Keldon Johnson (3) splits two defenders on his way to the basket against the Portland Trail Blazers.

SAN ANTONIO
44
bullets
41

CHAPTER FOUR

EARNING THEIR SPURS

One of George Gervin's four NBA scoring titles was a close call. April 9, 1978, was the final day of the NBA season. Gervin was locked in a duel for the league points lead with Denver Nuggets guard David Thompson. Heading into the day, Gervin was slightly ahead. But Thompson scored 73 points for the Nuggets in an early game. At the time, it was the third-highest point total in NBA history. Thompson also scored 32 points in the first quarter to set a record.

Gervin's Spurs had qualified for the playoffs. He didn't even need to play against the New Orleans Jazz. But he did, and he put on a show. Gervin needed 58 points to take the title back. By halftime he had poured in 53. Of those, 33 came in the second quarter. He broke Thompson's record for one quarter, set only hours earlier. Gervin scored 10 more points in the third quarter. With the scoring title in his pocket, he sat

George Gervin averaged 26.3 points per game during his 12 seasons with the Spurs in both the ABA and the NBA.

out the fourth. His final average was 27.22 points per game. Thompson's was 27.15.

David Robinson enjoyed a similar experience with San Antonio on April 24, 1994. Once again, this memorable moment in Spurs history took place on the final day of the regular season.

Aiming to win the 1993–94 scoring title, Robinson scored 71 points. That was a new franchise record. He also became the first NBA player to score at least 70 points in a game since Thompson, in his duel with Gervin 16 years earlier. With his scoring outburst, "the Admiral" narrowly beat out Orlando Magic star Shaquille O'Neal for the scoring title.

"There are times when you get in [the] zone and that was one of them," Robinson said during a question-and-answer session on Twitter in 2020. "I felt unstoppable. [The] scoring title was on the line so I was motivated."

FIVE TITLES, FIVE CLINCHERS

When they drafted Duncan, the Spurs had never won an NBA championship. Two years later, the towering young forward led them to the top. But he had a little help from the team's smallest player, 5-foot-10-inch Avery Johnson.

On June 25, 1999, the Spurs were locked in a close contest with the New York Knicks in Game 5 of the NBA Finals. Duncan

The Spurs celebrate their first NBA title after defeating the New York Knicks in the 1999 NBA Finals.

had 31 points and nine rebounds in the game, but the Spurs trailed 77–76 with 47 seconds remaining.

Johnson was the team's point guard. He had bounced around the league with four teams before sticking with San Antonio in the mid-1990s. Coach Gregg Popovich loved Johnson's intelligent play. In Game 5, Johnson rewarded his coach with a big shot. Spurs forward Sean Elliott spotted

Johnson open in the corner. Johnson drilled the shot to give San Antonio the lead. Neither team scored the rest of the night. The Spurs were NBA champions for the first time.

Four years later, San Antonio was back on top. This time Duncan was the clinching game's undisputed star. He racked up 21 points, 20 rebounds, 10 assists, and eight blocks in an 88–77 Game 6 win over the New Jersey Nets.

Even those stats didn't get Duncan most of the attention. That went to Robinson, who was playing his final NBA game. He went out in style, with 13 points, 17 rebounds, and two blocked shots. Robinson retired as a two-time champion, but Duncan was just getting started.

Two years later, the Spurs were champions again. On June 23, 2005, they needed seven games to oust the Detroit Pistons in the Finals. Duncan led the way, scoring 25 points with 11 rebounds. Manu Ginobili chipped in 23 points and four assists in the clinching win.

The Memorial Day Miracle

In the final seconds of Game 2 of the 1999 Western Conference finals, Sean Elliott took an inbounds pass near the right corner. Slightly off-balance, he tiptoed over the sideline and made a game-winning three-pointer to defeat the Portland Trail Blazers. The shot became known as "the Memorial Day Miracle."

Forward Manu Ginobili's strong play in Game 7 helped the Spurs defeat the Detroit Pistons in the 2005 NBA Finals.

Becky Hammon

San Antonio had won a title in five games (1999), six games (2003), and seven games (2005). The only thing missing was a four-game sweep. The Spurs took care of that on June 14, 2007, as they eliminated the Cleveland Cavaliers 83–82. San Antonio wrapped up its fourth title in nine seasons.

The Spurs were not done yet, although they had to wait seven years to win title number five. After losing to the Miami Heat in the 2013 Finals, San Antonio got its revenge on June 15, 2014. The Spurs defeated the Heat that night 104–87 in Game 5 of the Finals. Kawhi Leonard shone with 22 points and 10 rebounds. The Spurs captured the fifth championship in franchise history.

Point guard Tony Parker reflected after the Spurs' latest title: "We're a true team."

Tony Parker holds up the Larry O'Brien Trophy as the Spurs celebrate their 2014 NBA championship.

TIMELINE

1967

The Dallas Chaparrals, who later become the San Antonio Spurs, begin play as one of 11 teams in the inaugural American Basketball Association (ABA).

1973

The franchise moves from Dallas to San Antonio and undergoes a name change from the Chaparrals to the Spurs.

1976

The ABA merges with the NBA. Four ABA teams, including the Spurs, join the NBA.

1987

San Antonio selects David Robinson, a center from Navy, with the top pick in the NBA Draft.

1993

Owner Red McCombs sells the Spurs to a group of investors, led by Peter Holt, for $75 million.

1996

General manager Gregg Popovich fires coach Bob Hill and names himself Spurs coach.

1997

San Antonio selects Wake Forest big man Tim Duncan with the first pick in the NBA Draft.

1999

The Spurs defeat the New York Knicks for the first championship in franchise history.

2002

The Spurs move into the SBC Center, now known as the AT&T Center.

2003

The Spurs defeat the New Jersey Nets to win their second NBA title.

2005

The Spurs edge the Detroit Pistons in Game 7 to win their third NBA championship.

2007

The Spurs sweep LeBron James and the Cleveland Cavaliers to win title number four.

2013

The Spurs squander a late lead in Game 6 of the NBA Finals before falling to the Miami Heat in Game 7.

2014

The Spurs avenge the 2013 NBA Finals series loss by crushing the Heat for their fifth title.

2016

Duncan retires from the NBA after playing 19 seasons, all with the Spurs.

2022

Popovich becomes the NBA's all-time winningest head coach, earning win number 1,336.

FRANCHISE HISTORY
Dallas Chaparrals (1967–70; 1971–73) (ABA)
Texas Chaparrals (1970–71) (ABA)
San Antonio Spurs (1973–76) (ABA)
San Antonio Spurs (1976–) (NBA)

NBA CHAMPIONSHIPS
1999, 2003, 2005, 2007, 2014

KEY PLAYERS
LaMarcus Aldridge (2015–21)
Bruce Bowen (2001–09)
Tim Duncan (1997–2016)
Sean Elliott (1989–93; 1994–2001)
George Gervin (1974–85)
Artis Gilmore (1982–87)
Manu Ginobili (2002–18)
Avery Johnson (1991, 1992–93, 1994–2001)
Larry Kenon (1975–80)
Kawhi Leonard (2011–18)
Mike Mitchell (1981–88)
Tony Parker (2001–18)
Alvin Robertson (1984–89)
David Robinson (1989–2003)
James Silas (1972–81)

KEY COACHES
Stan Albeck (1980–83)
Larry Brown (1988–92)
Doug Moe (1976–80)
Gregg Popovich (1996   )

HOME ARENAS
State Fair Coliseum (1967–73)
Moody Coliseum (1967–73)
Tarrant County Coliseum (1970–71)
Lubbock Municipal Coliseum (1970–71)
HemisFair Arena (1973–93)
Alamodome (1993–2002)
AT&T Center (2002–)
Formerly known as: SBC Center (2002–2006)

TEAM TRIVIA

TOUGH NEGOTIATIONS

When the Spurs were trying to trade for George Gervin in 1974, the negotiations resulted in a lot of arguing. In fact, things got so ugly that Gervin went into hiding for a week while the teams and the ABA league office hammered out the deal.

LONGEVITY

Gregg Popovich began his 24th season as head coach of the Spurs on opening night of the 2019–20 season. No NBA coach had ever been with one team longer.

TROPHY CASE

Tim Duncan is one of only five players to win NBA Finals MVP at least three times. The others are Michael Jordan (six), LeBron James (four), Earvin "Magic" Johnson (three), and Shaquille O'Neal (three). Seven other players have won it twice, including Kawhi Leonard, who won with the Spurs in 2014 and the Toronto Raptors in 2019.

ACROSS THE POND

In 2007 the Spurs' Tony Parker became the first European-born player to win NBA Finals MVP.

GLOSSARY

assist
A pass that leads directly to a basket.

draft
A system that allows teams to acquire new players coming into a league.

dynasty
A team that has an extended period of success, usually winning multiple championships in the process.

franchise
A sports organization, including the top-level team and all minor league affiliates.

general manager
An executive who runs a team and is responsible for finding and signing players.

merge
To join with another to create something new, such as a company, a team, or a league.

rebound
To catch the ball after a shot has been missed.

retire
To end one's career.

rookie
A professional athlete in his or her first year of competition.

two-way
Possessing skill on both offense and defense.

veteran
A player who has played for many years.

BOOKS

Flynn, Brendan. *The NBA Encyclopedia for Kids*. Minneapolis, MN: Abdo Publishing, 2022.

Mahoney, Brian. *GOATs of Basketball*. Minneapolis, MN: Abdo Publishing, 2022.

Ybarra, Andres. *Great Basketball Debates*. Minneapolis, MN: Abdo Publishing, 2019.

ONLINE RESOURCES

To learn more about the San Antonio Spurs, please visit **abdobooklinks.com** or scan this QR code. These links are routinely monitored and updated to provide the most current information available.

ABOUT THE AUTHOR

Drew Silverman is a freelance sportswriter based in Philadelphia, Pennsylvania. He graduated from Syracuse University and has worked for ESPN, Comcast SportsNet, and NBC Sports. He also was sports editor of the *Bulletin* newspaper in Philadelphia. He lives in Philadelphia with his wife and two children.